The Power of a Thought

Danny Vickers

THE POWER OF A THOUGHT

Printed in the United States of America
ISBN: 978-1-7347494-6-5 (Paperback)
ISBN: 978-1-7347494-7-2 (Digital)
Library of Congress Control Number: 2020916431

Published by Cocoon to Wings Publishing
7810 Gall Blvd, #311
Zephyrhills, FL 33541
www.StephanieOutten.com
(813) 906-WING (9464)

Cover design by ETP Creative

The Power of a Thought

Contents

Foreword

I am honored to write this foreword for my brother in Christ, Danny Vickers. As the CEO and Chief Publishing Officer of Cocoon to Wings Publishing, I have had the privilege of working with many new and existing authors to birth their "literary baby."

While I have only known Elder Danny, as I refer to him because he is one of the elders of my church, Center for Manifestation in Tampa, Florida, for a short time, I have grown fond of his teaching, his character, and his mindset when it comes to powerful thinking to live a purposeful life.

When he approached my business about this book, The Power of a Thought, I was immediately intrigued. There was a time when my own thoughts did not line up with the vision I saw for my life. I knew God had a positive trajectory for me, but I couldn't see past my present situations. My thoughts became negative. Therefore, everything around me either felt negative or actually became negative.

There's the saying, "You are what you eat." Well, I began to realize that you are what you think. If you think unconstructive, damaging, and ineffectual thoughts, what will you become? Unconstructive, damaged, and ineffectual. Our Heavenly Father did not create us to have these useless thoughts. We have the mind of Christ. So, our thoughts are His thoughts, and His thoughts are always good. Philippians 4:8 in the New Living Translation in the dressing room talking to her from the other side of the door, the Lord gave me a thought to start developing a relationship with my shoppers so that I could not only help them with their outer appearance, but I could also help them uncover their inner beauty. From that thought, my first business, Eternal Style, Inc. was born. That one dressing room encounter sparked a thought that turned into a business. That business gave me a new purpose, but it also helped me recognize that I was also hiding behind the clothes.

My own thoughts about myself were not pure, loving, kind, true or admirable. I did not love myself, but I sure let the clothes make me think I did. Fast forward more than 20 years to where I am today. My thoughts of myself have completely transformed. I had to do the soul work, that deep inner cleansing of my soul, in order to form new thoughts that would allow me to now be successful in this new business, my ministry - Cocoon to Wings Publishing. Now, rather than helping women use clothing to help them change their image, I coach women, men, and children through the process of transformative writing to heal their souls. As a Literary Doula™ and publisher, my passion is to help individuals bring forth stories that will leave a lasting legacy on this earth. My own thoughts had to change in order for me to effectively support others as their writing coach and publisher.

The Kingdom is crying out for people to practice right thinking. Elder Danny was born to help people be transformed by renewing their mind, as we are told to do in Romans 12:2. Elder Danny keeps his thoughts centered on the things of God and what he is supposed to do to help elevate the minds of God's people. He practices what he teaches and gives useful, easy-to-apply tools to help people understand the power of their thoughts. When there is poor thinking, that begins to actualize in the way we live. Danny Vickers is a man who will not stand by and allow God's children to wallow in a negative mindset. He believes, like Ephesians 4:22-24, that we are to put off our old sinful nature (negative, lowly thinking) and let the Spirit renew our thoughts and attitudes. We were created to be like Christ, and our thoughts and actions should align with our new nature (positive, powerful, life changing thinking).

Our thoughts should elevate us and those around us. If you notice that your thoughts are deflating, keeping you in bondage, causing you not to see your dreams and visions for your life come to pass, spend a little time with Danny Vickers and you will begin to see that change. He will encourage you, talk with you about your thoughts, dig deep to find out what you are thinking on and how those thoughts have fueled you or failed you. He will design a plan for you, much of which he has already given you in this power-packed book. He will help you set your thoughts on things above so that you can live your life with purpose, intention, and God's divine grace.

I hope this book will bless you and set you on the path to powerful, right thinking. The seeds of your dreams, visions, and purpose are all waiting to manifest. They need you to pour Christ-centered, positive thoughts on them so they can grow. Using the tools Elder Danny so freely offers will help change the course of your life and allow you to fully understand The Power of a Thought.

Stephanie Outten

CEO | Chief Publishing Officer | Literary Doula™ | Transformation Agent & Bestselling Author
Cocoon to Wings Publishing, LLC

The Birth of "Danvino DaVision"

Back in the early '90s, the company operations manager had sent me a message on my communicator pager device that read, "Come see me after you finish your route before you leave and go home today." Well, I began to sweat bullets like blood. I was wondering what in the hell I had done so bad to get a write-up or, even worse, to be fired after a year of hard laboring work throwing cases of beer all day in a hot truck with no air conditioning.

So now, I became mad and built up malicious anger in my mind. *What is he going to pin down on me this time?* In my mind, they were going to take some more money out of my check, saying I was short of products and some beer cases. Sad to say, I became the first "Black Panther" ready to defend myself like Chadwick Boseman's character, T'Challa, in the movie. By that time, I was in ready mode, so I knocked on his door, entered his office, and sat down.

Mr. Tony pulled up in his chair with both of his elbows on his big fancy office table and said, "Every customer that you service on this route is so well pleased with you and the sales numbers have doubled up, so we decided to promote you to become the first African-American sales route director because of your strong customer service skills." **Mr. Tony** stood up and came around, hugged me, shook my hand, and said, "Congratulations! Welcome to the sales team. And oh, by the way, you have been assigned a company vehicle as well."

I had put on all of that angry armor for nothing. I felt so convicted that I broke down and cried in his arms. For the first time, I felt so well respected and important in my life as a young black man.

▲▼

On Monday morning, I got to wear my shirt and tie on my first day as the new sales director with a company car. I was so excited that I immediately drove over to **Mr. Vino Vitaly's** liquor store to share the good news. **Mr. Vino** always had some type of story to tell me about when he was in the mafia gang, but I believe some of it was lies because his wife used to smirk or roll her eyes at him whenever he told the stories. I sat there and listened out of respect, but I had to admit they were pretty entertaining stories.

I believe **Mr. Vitaly** had pretty much adopted me in his heart like a son. That old Italian friend of mine always spoke life into my future. I believe **Mr. Vino** may have been the reason why I was promoted. He was the first man in my life that saw something in me that I didn't see in myself as a young black man. For some reason, for years, he called me Danvino.

One Christmas Eve, I asked him why he called me **Danvino**. **Mr. Vitaly** slowly put his hand on my shoulder, and he said, "Use da-vision." I clearly understood what he was trying to say. **Use my vision**. Now, as I reflect on that moment, it always makes me smile with a chuckle or two. Well, so sad to say, but my heavy bourbon-drinker-on-the-rocks friend who loved his **Cohiba Cigars** passed away at the age of 87 shortly after the new year of 1992. Boy, how I surely miss that old man and his amazing Godfather stories.

▲▼

God placed this vision in my heart in 2015 to start a podcast, and the only name that kept coming to me was **Danvino DaVision Podcast.** It finally made sense. I believe **Mr. Vino Vitaly** spoke this into the future of 2020 for me.

My dedication to you, **Mr. Vino Vitaly**, my Italian friend, who I love and miss dearly: Rest in Peace to The Storytelling Italian King - 1992.

Chapter 1

The Empire State Building Was Birthed From a Thought

One day a certain man woke up with an idea of thought, and he started up a small business. The business turned into a corporation, and the corporation became an executive Fortune 500 company. The idea from this one thought has become The Empire State Building. I ask you, what are your thoughts, and how far can you take your thoughts?

> **Proverbs 29:18** - *"Where there is no vision, the people perish: but he that keep the law, happy is he."*

On March 17, 1930, the construction of the Empire State Building began under the direction of architect firm Shreve, Lamb & Harmon Associates. The framework rose four and a half stories per week. On May 1, 1931, President Hoover pressed the button called, "It's okay to build" and approved the start.

Most people know what the Empire State Building looks like. If you don't, I would recommend you do an internet search to see its magnificence. This building used to be the tallest in New York until someone came up with a bigger and taller thought and constructed The Twin Towers. Unfortunately, terrorists had the evil thought on September 11, 2001 to bring The Twin Towers down.

Do you have a powerful thought that needs to be built? One that even evil can't destroy.

Let's keep this in mind. Everybody does not have the thoughts of God to build with a purpose. Some people around you have their own agendas and want to tear down your dreams and keep you from fulfilling your purpose by speaking evil words against you. They can't see or understand why God did not show it to them. So now I ask, what are you trying to build before God?

> **Matthew 16:18** - *"And I say also unto thee, That thou art Peter, and upon this rock I will build my church; and the gates of hell shall not prevail against it."*

In the scripture above, imagine replacing the word "church" with "thoughts." God gave us the mind of His thoughts. He turned his thoughts into rocks, and the rocks became stones. The stones became bricks, and the bricks have now become a realization of a place where man can dwell.

To me, a thought is like an eagle with a plan. First, the eagle becomes pregnant, and then she starts building a home known as a nest. Once the nest is built, the eagle can then lay her eggs. Now, in the proper nature of time, the eaglets will be hatched out of their shells, and one day in the development of time, they will begin to live the life of an eagle. God impregnated us with a thought of the idea, and He will give us the instructions on how to build the nest to hold the thoughts of His vision He has imparted to us so that it can become a reality.

#1Pregnant

#2 Egg

#3 Life

It all came from

The Power of a Thought.

Chapter 2

10 Powerful Points About the Thoughts & Visions Within You

> **Habakkuk 2:2** - *"And the Lord answered me, and said, Write the vision, and make it plain upon tables, that he may run that readeth it."*

1. You must continually keep the vision God gives you in your heart and your mind. It's very important that you write the

vision down and make it plain on tablets (your notebook, computer, phone - wherever you write information that others can read) so that those who read it with a kindred spirit will be able to see and understand the vision. You should bring them in as partners accordingly to their skills and their abilities. This new partner can now become focused and clear on how to help you bring God's plan to fruition.

2. A powerful thought will require you to build up uncommon strength and patience. As an example, when someone close to you betrays you like Judas did with Jesus, you can develop an uncommon strength to forgive as Jesus did with Judas. Jesus didn't let his thoughts be clouded with Judas' betrayal. He patiently stayed focused on his vision and purpose. That's what He desires of us, too. He wants us to build uncommon strength

and patience to bring our positive and powerful thoughts to pass.

3. The power of a thought must be born within your mind. Your thoughts cannot be borrowed from other people because other people's thoughts become your opinions. You cannot build an empire without the proper manual that comes with instructions. Remember, only you and you alone will receive the confirmation from God for the correct instructions on how to develop the thought birthed within you. King David had no one else to encourage him, but he believed the powerful thought that God birthed within his soul. King David became an uncommon king because his thoughts were to follow God and not concern himself with the thoughts of others. He allowed God to lead his thoughts so that he could be the type of king Israel needed.

4. The power of your thoughts will qualify those who deserve access to you. So many people will reach for you, but it is important that you qualify those who are called by God to have access to your visions and your thoughts. Jesus never went home with Pharisees and Sadducees, the so-called "Important Men." But yet, Jesus had an entire meal with Zacchaeus, the tax collector. Not everyone is for you, so your thoughts and visions should not be shared with everyone. They are reserved only for those God called to have access to them.

5. God is committed to the thoughts that He birthed within you, whether you embrace it now or later. Peter made continuous mistakes, and Jesus said to Peter, "But I have prayed for thee, that thy faith fail not: and when thou art converted, strengthen thy brethren." **Luke 22:32**

6. It is very important that you learn how to protect the thoughts that God gives you. It requires you to have that uncommon favor with other people. Joseph received favor from Potiphar and Pharaoh. Esther received favor from the king. Ruth received favor from Boaz. When the hand of God is upon you, favor will come. You must sow into it; you need to expect it and protect it.

7. The power of your thoughts will require deep passion. Passion is energy, enthusiasm, and strength. Passion is a clue to the path of the Holy Spirit that has been chosen for your life. Now, it is possible to have a passion for something unholy, but you must recognize that any thoughts toward achievement will require the Godly thoughts of passion from God. If you want to know what your gift is, look behind your passion. My passion was always

entertainment and comedy from childhood to adulthood. God anointed me to become someone that could filter myself without offending people, but also bringing them joy and happiness through my personality and words. I have a unique way of helping others identify their negative thoughts and get them to accept them and laugh about them. This is because I have a deep passion for this that was imparted to me by the Holy Spirit.

8. Some thoughts can come from pain. Some people who were raised in poverty will often develop a passion for helping other people to become prosperous. Some people live with a disease or some sort of a health problem or handicap, and they become obsessed with helping others to develop great health. What pain are your thoughts coming from?

9. The power of your thoughts requires the power of faith. If you've read biographies of famous, successful people, you may have been able to identify how their own powerful thoughts led to their achievements. And those achievements nurtured the seed of faith that became a raging force within them. Like Bill Gates - everyone in IBM's boardroom thought his idea was crazy. I share the story of this later in the book. But, the power of his thought allowed him to execute on his vision, and that vision made him a billionaire.

10. There is danger in having a weak focus. One reason why someone may fail is because of broken focus. You will succeed when you allow something to consume you. When God gives you the thought of power, it will require all of your time, your love, and energy. So, you must be willing

to pour and invest everything into that thought to bring it to manifestation.

Chapter 3

Ten Powerful Thoughts of a Vision Within You

1. If you pick up a book each month for a year, and you read about the same subject and learn about it from 12 different authors, your four seasons of learning within that year will increase your chances of being more knowledgeable about that topic than most of the individuals within your community. You can become a problem solver for the future.

2. Having a broken thought means you are not sure within yourself. You have a lack of faith in yourself, in God, and in your abilities. The spirit of procrastination comes when you are not sure in yourself, and it hinders the vision God placed in you.

3. The power of your thoughts will require strong preparation. Jesus prepared for 30 years just to do three years of ministry. Some people call it short-term pain for life-term gain. Remember, it takes only 12 hours to build a Toyota, but it takes six months to build a Rolls-Royce. Are you a Toyota or a Rolls-Royce?

4. When you announce your thoughts, visions, and dreams, a few who believe in you will be encouraged and excited to assist you. Your idea has now activated them to become in a relationship with

their gift and their calling. Define their position and release them to work.

5. When you announce your vision, those who are tempted to oppose you may decide to join you because of your determination. When you're a leader, you don't recruit. People follow you because they see what you are doing is a great cause. Jesus ended up with 70 disciples because he was a leader that shared his vision. But only 12 stayed because they understood and were willing to follow the vision.

6. When people are assisting you, then you should always feed them with the wisdom of God, knowledge, and the understanding of leadership. Keep a list of your top 12 key partners. This is so necessary to complete the vision within you. I have a few biblical tips on why you should focus on the number 12. In the Old Testament,

God used 12 tribes to develop His plan and vision. Jesus used 12 disciples. The New Jerusalem has 12 gates. Define your expectations of these 12 partners. Plan a reward for their participation as often as you can.

7. Remember, the vision came from God, and He put it in your thoughts. That's why it will require the miracles of God to build that vision. God would never birth a dream within you that is achievable without Him. He gives you His vision and dreams to keep you connected to Him and to perpetuate His plans and desires. It will require Him to complete it, and when it's done, He will get the glory. Everybody that survived through a miscarriage or abortion, but still made it to Earth. God hid his seed inside of you. You were created to live. The purpose of a seed is to come up if nothing hinders

it. With the right fertilizer, you can be a tree that produces good fruit.

8. The thoughts of your vision will determine what you do first each morning, and your obsession will control the use of your time. Every morning when you wake up, you have an opportunity to give your first fruits to God before you do anything else. Give your thoughts to God as your first fruits. Command your thoughts to be led by the Holy Spirit and watch how that shifts things for you.

9. The thoughts of your vision will require so much strength and wise use of your time. The bigger your dream, the more it will require you to invest your time and energy. Become time conscious and energy motivated because when people see how passionate you are, they will

become excited about joining or partnering with you.

10. When you write your vision down and make it plain, you just create an awesome bond with those who have a similar desire and goal that was birthed within them as well.

Chapter 4

The Adversary & Objective

Are you attracted to your assignment?

God created and planted a seed of **assignment** within every man. Within your **assignment**, there is a hidden solution to a problem that you are called to solve.

Mr. Henry Ford would have never thought that his vision of making and designing the first moving automobile would have spearheaded the idea of heavy transportation on wheels, which solved the problems of trading goods and transporting products all around the world.

The very purpose of your assignment is to solve a problem for people who are stuck with a problem and in need of an answer. Trust me when I say this, "You have the key answers to the problems of some people, and they will bless you, openly reward you, and change your life for the rest of your life because of your good work in helping them solve their problems.

Here's a little-known secret to help you: Stay in the lane that God told you to drive in. Stay in your purpose and let others stay in theirs.

> **1 Corinthians 7:20** - *"Let every man abide in the same calling wherein he was called."*

When your assignment is overlooked and not recognized, you are not celebrated. When you're not celebrated, you are not rewarded.

One of the most tormented places to be on Earth is to be uncelebrated by the people you live with, go to church and fellowship with, or work with.

There is nothing more disturbing on Earth than the torment of living a life unrewarded when you have the gift lying dormant within you. If they can just hear and trust you, they will become free from bondage.

Chapter 5

Ten Points You Need to Know About Your Assignment

1. Your assignment is always for you to serve the people that celebrate you and speak what says the Lord to the people that tolerate you. **Jeremiah 1:7** "...for thou shalt go to all that I shall send thee, and whatsoever I command thee thou shalt speak."

2. Your assignment from God comes with suffering and demonic attacks. Whenever you stand before people and make the announcement of the assignment God called you to, all hell breaks loose on you and your assignment. The devil in hell can't stop it, but he would like to slow down your progress. Here's how Paul described his assignment as a preacher, teacher, and Apostle. **Timothy 1:12.** "For the which cause I also suffer these things: nevertheless, I am not ashamed: for I know whom I have believed, and am persuaded that he is able to keep that which I have committed unto Him against that day."

3. What is it that worries you so badly and troubles your spirit to the point that you are uncomfortable? This just may be about your assignment. You may be called to **heal and restore** the people of God.

Nehemiah was in a good place, and he had a great job and position. He was living in the King's Palace, and the King gave Nehemiah favor and loved him. Nehemiah got some disturbing news about the suffering of his people in need of rebuilding the walls of Jerusalem. When the people of Judah were attacked, their enemy came in and tore down their walls. By tearing down their walls, the enemy got to the people. They burned down the camp. The people of Judah rebuilt the camp but didn't know how to build the wall again. They lost their hedge of protection, and that hedge is what made them comfortable.

4. Your thoughts will continue to contain the greatest gifts of your passion and purpose, which will lead you into wisdom, strength, and understanding.

5. When I see a certain purpose and passion that keeps traveling through the thoughts of a man's mind, I know that he is in his place of assignment. Here's a tip: whatever you love, you will seek the wisdom of God to build it.

6. The proof of a powerful, effective thought is the investment of time you put back in it. When I see you are willing to invest your time, I know exactly what you love and are passionate about. That is your assignment.

7. You should always keep your vision and your future assignment embedded into the geographical places that you are called to. God wants you to mark the spot where you are now and allow Him to order your steps to where you are going. Remember, God said, "A good man's steps are ordered by the Lord." Geography matters so much

because it puts you into the flow of favor of God.

8. Keep in mind someone is watching you at all times. I was talking to a good friend of mine, Ms. Tyeesha Holt. She is so anointed in public speaking. In her book, *Nothing Gay About Being Gay*, she uses her words to help change the lives of people who are struggling with leaving a lifestyle of homosexuality. Ms. Holt is a great example of someone who is flowing in her assignment geographically, and she's in the place where God has called her to be. As she continues to grow in wisdom and gets more understanding, she will become stronger in mastering her gifts. I said one day to her, "Ms. Holt, you are one person away from meeting the person who God will use to bless you and change your life for the rest of your life." An elderly mother in church used to

quote this old wise saying to me: "Who sees you determines who God can use to promote you." That's a quote I will always remember. I will remain steadfast to my gifts and my calling and stay unmovable through all of my adversities because God will make me victorious.

9. Your assignment is in the hands of a Master Cooking Chef. It will require seasons of preparation. You must keep studying the ways of God so that you can rightly divide the Word of Truth (2 Timothy 2:15). You will experience seasons of insignificance, isolation, waiting, warfare, persecution, injustice, silence, and promotions. Jesus invested 30 years of preparation for only three years of ministry to teach and train His disciples.

10. Your assignment will always come with enemies. Jesus declared that the servant

is not above his Lord. "If the world hates you, you know that it has hated Me before *it hated* you." "...A slave is not greater than his master. If they persecuted Me, they will also persecute you." **John 15:18, 20.** Please understand that your enemies are very necessary for your life just as well as your friends. Your friends provide comfort; your enemy provides elevation and promotion for you. If you look back on some of the lives of the greatest men and women, you will find that they all have similar stories to tell about how important enemies can be. Recognizing your assignment will dry your tears, unload your burdens, and restore the joy into your countenance.

Chapter 6

Knowing Your Personal Limitations

Stop trying to be everybody's superhero. You can't save everyone. You can only do what God created you to do through the gifts and the skills that have been given to you by God.

> **Matthew 25:14-15** - *"For the kingdom of heaven is as a man travelling into a far country, who called his own servants, and delivered unto them his goods. And unto*

> *one he gave five talents, to another he gave two, and to another he gave one; to every man* **according to his** *several* **ability**; *and straightway took his journey."*

The keyword is ability. God will not place more on you than you can bear. Now, most men will place unmeasurable burdens and pressure on you, and you may not be anointed to handle it. That's why you must know what you can or cannot do.

Don't be afraid to say **NO** sometimes. So many people have lost great business empires along with great partnerships, awesome employees, and close family members because they were pushed beyond their limits.

An inexperienced minister that is not quite following the instructions of the Holy Spirit of God can mislead people with unwise counsel by trying to do more than what they were specifically asked to do. They did not recognize their limitations.

An inexperienced quarterback in the NFL running the football without someone in front of him to keep him protected from receiving a lifetime injury may cost him his career.

An inexperienced aircraft pilot will crash a plane if he or she fails to recognize their limitations.

You can have unlimited passion, but make sure you are well equipped with the right instructions.

Five Facts About Knowing Your Personal Limitations

1. Almighty God created your life, and He surrounded you with others who want to team up with you and have a partnership with your vision. Arrogance deprives

you of the incredible contribution others desire to give.

2. If you fail to recognize or understand your personal limitations, you will become blind to the hidden gift within you and to those around you.

3. If you learn to know your limitations, you will have the ability to discern the right contacts and the opportunities around you.

4. Most times, we have to let someone know that our limitations don't meet their requests or their requirements. You can have unlimited passion, but make sure you are well equipped with the right instructions.

Chapter 7

The Human Body of Remarkable Seeds Hidden Within You

So many of us don't realize the seed gifts of what we contain within us. We waste so much time studying what we lost and what we could have done differently instead of taking inventory of what we have been given. It becomes tragic beyond words. Whatever we receive from God, we are to plant it within the lives of others.

Take a very long and hard look at what you are called to be and be thankful for the seed gift you have already been given. We all possess something that is the key to a solution for the future.

What makes you think of extraordinary thoughts?

The answer is God. The body that He created for you contains multiple seeds that work differently from any other seeds that you hold and contain within your body. Here's the good news: they all work together (seeds), and they all have a different assignment for your good.

Let me give you an example. Everything you are comes from God. Your ability to see, touch, taste, and smell are just a small portion of the seeds that have been given to you. There are other seeds God has hidden deep within you that will begin to sprout only when He has deemed you worthy to operate within that gift for a specific purpose.

Each seed has a different purpose, but they all work together just to operate and function in one body. The seeds within you are so powerful, and if your seeds ever come out of you, they will produce fruits in the land of God and draw people to the salvation of God.

The Bible said, "Be fruitful and multiply."

Most people always talk about the seed of an idea that comes to their thoughts but never do anything to make it a reality. This is one of the most vital principles you must understand in unleashing a harvest of seeds. When you start releasing the seeds of God within you, you are showing the evidence of your faith that God will provide for you.

Whenever you talk about an idea of seed thoughts that God placed in your mind, and you never do anything, you are guaranteed another season of nothing for your future.

When you only learn to plant and sow the seeds that God planted within you into yourself, and you do not plant them into others, you have now become living proof of mastering the meaning of greed.

The spirit of greed comes from Satan because he knows what would happen if you started planting your seeds in the Earth. A good harvest will bring you a good life and living a good life will bring you into an abundant life in Christ Jesus.

Chapter 8

The Seven Facts of Good Connections

1. A good connection may not always come from someone close to you. Remember the story of the butler who forgot all about Joseph for two years? Pharaoh, the Egyptian king, kept having disturbing dreams that stimulated his memory. There was a problem of an unhappy dreaming king that was sitting on the throne of Egypt, and it needed to be solved in the land of the Egyptians.

2. The butler was not a friend of Joseph; that's why it was so easy for him to forget about Joseph after having spent time with him in prison. Pharaoh was angry every day because he could not interpret the meaning of his dreams, and it had a bad effect on everyone in the palace. Can you imagine everybody trying to find the solution to heal the king? The council contacted the top psychic palm readers, magicians, and astrologers. The butler, all of a sudden, remembered the gift of Joseph. This dream interpreter helped him solve his dream because he had the same problem that Pharaoh was having. Joseph's gift was used for the Lord in his life. God used the butler to connect Joseph to Pharaoh.

3. Some connections in your future are only for a moment and not a lifetime. Philip, in the Book of Acts, came in contact with

and connected to an Ethiopian eunuch, and yet we never read or heard of them meeting back up again. They never had any other relationship again after their conversation about how to receive Jesus as Lord. Read **Acts 8** in your bible. This one interaction was only for that moment, and that moment was for the eunuch to receive the Lord and become baptized. As soon as he was baptized, the Lord carried Philip away, and the eunuch became born again.

4. In most cases, you may need to pursue a connection. Remember, Naomi was the connection between Ruth and Boaz. Ruth pursued Naomi. Ruth said to her, "Entreat me not to leave thee, or to return from following after thee: for wither thou goest, I will go, and where thou lodgest, I will lodge: thy people shall be my people, and thy God my God:" **Ruth 1:16.**

5. Some connections in your life may distract and discourage you from having a relationship with them. If you read the Book of Ruth, you will see how Naomi tried so hard to instruct Ruth away from her. Naomi said to Ruth, "...return thou after thy sister in law." **Ruth 1:15.** But, Ruth refused to accept any discouragement. She was persistent in learning and following Naomi. Why? Because Ruth knew that her destiny was tied to Naomi.

6. There are people around you who will try to stop you from having that connection. Here is another great biblical story to help you understand this. There was a blind man that was crying out to Jesus, but he was being distracted and instructed by the people around him to keep silent. But this blind man knew he might never get this opportunity again. He cried out so loud to Jesus until He heard his cry

within the multitude of the people. The blind man's voice came from the root of his heart because he needed the connection of a miracle to change his life for the rest of his life. He refused to let the people around him stop what he was striving for, and that was purpose.

7. God gave you a good mind and a consciousness to have the responsibility to recognize your connection. It's not always their responsibility to recognize you. The woman with the issue of blood recognized Jesus. Jesus did not recognize her until after she showed great faith and healing. **Mark 5:25-34.**

8. There will always be someone who despises your relationship to your connection. Sometimes, your enemy may be a silent one. You may not even know that someone is your enemy. So, if you have

a good connection right now in your life, Satan will stir someone up to break the relationship. Sometimes it's good to go through what I like to call "test" connections; it helps you to realize whether or not the bond and trust with each other in business or relationship is real.

Chapter 9

Your Thoughts Have A Short Gift of Time

I have studied the biographies of a poor man's thinking vs. a man with prosperous thoughts, dreams, and visions. The major difference between the prosperous people and the poor is their value of time. I sometimes drive through a low-income housing area, sometimes referred to as "The Hood." I always see healthy, strong men and women casually drinking, smoking, sitting on the steps of a porch, or hanging on the corner of a mom and pop store for hours. By repeating this habit for so long, they get so used to their environment of wastefulness that they become physically and mentally challenged. They have now chosen to waste and invest their time in trivial things, while other people with determination and a prosperous mindset are working on a business or the next great idea. There are two major decisions that you can make in your life that will either shift you into a poverty mindset or a healthy, wise prosperous mindset - waste time or value it and use it to your advantage.

The Difference is the Management of Time.

The five facts you should know about managing your time.

1. Whenever there is something so significant and important for you to accomplish, it will require a lot of your time and investment in it.

2. Preparation requires time, and that preparation will bring quality value to the products or services you produce, in turn bringing you long-range financial rewards.

3. You will receive an overwhelming overflow of unapologetic favorable, wealth, and riches based on the measure of energy that you pour into one of your great thoughts. God sees the energy you put forth, and He will reward you for it.

4. Making successful negotiations will always require the investment of time. Those who can overcome the temptation of not being in a rush will always be in control of their transactions.

5. It is so imperative that you teach those around you how to respect your time, and likewise, you must do the same for them as well. It frustrates me when someone makes an appointment with me and

doesn't call when they know that they won't make it. I can get my money back, but I can't get back my time. You just cost me. You must live with great integrity; it will build good character within you.

The five facts on making your time count.

1. Keep a vision board or a visual list of your thoughts, dreams, and goals before you at all times.

2. Time is precious; that's why you should establish a time limit on every appointment. If I host an event from 1 PM to 3 PM, I will start on time, and I will end it on time. Why? Because my time is valuable, so I had to learn how to control my environment.

3. Recognize that your presence and your time are extremely valuable and fruitful to others. If you have the words of

wisdom within you, people will repeat exactly what they heard and learned from you and will share it with others to encourage them. I want those who are around me to treasure each moment and make that moment count by giving and sharing communication with me.

4. Keep a mark on those who consistently disrespect your time. If people don't value and respect your time, your wisdom will not be respected as well. The Bible says, "**Give not** that which is holy unto the **dogs**, neither **cast** ye your pearls before **swine**, lest they trample them under their feet and turn again and rend you." **Matthew 7:6.** That's why your time and your words are so valuable.

5. **Ecclesiastes 3:1.** "To everything there is a season, and a time to every purpose under the heaven:" **Ecclesiastes 3:17.**

"There is a time there for every purpose and for every work." **Ecclesiastes 5:15,16.** See then that ye walk circumspectly, not as fools, but as wise, Redeeming the time, because the days are evil." When you put your time into your gift, your productivity will be multiplied, and your financial worth will increase.

Chapter 10

The Enemy is Attracted to Your Gifts

Jesus always had enemies, and Jesus always recognized who His enemies were.

> **John 7:19** - *"Why do you go about in trying to kill me?"*

The Holy Spirit will always allow you to recognize the adversary around you.

1. The man with no integrity will hate you because you have good integrity before man and God.

2. The man with bad morals will hate you because you have good morals before man and God.

3. The man who lives in impurities will despise you because you live in pure purpose with good intentions before man and God.

4. The lazy man will despise you because you live and walk in diligence before man and God.

5. The religious man with a prideful heart will hate you because you have a relationship with God.

6. A man without the favor of God in his life will hate you because God shows you favor in your life.

7. A man with a dead soul who doesn't know the purpose of his life will try to find ways to manipulate you to cancel your purpose and abort your thoughts.

I have given you the seven most deadly reasons as to why your enemy hates you and why they want to stop you and destroy you. It is so imperative that you know your spiritual leader and are consciously aware of who God has assigned to teach and mentor you. You want to be paired with someone who holds you accountable and helps you reach and complete your assignment. I had to learn how to give up my life to God. God started teaching me how to find my life within him. **Matthew 10:39** Jesus said, "Whoever finds their life will lose it, and whoever loses their life for my sake will find it."

Now when you lose your life in Christ, you become planted and rooted in the good grounds of God. God gives you a specific assignment according to the measure of your faith and the great expectation He is calling you to. He reveals his purpose in you so you can become unleashed into your purpose like never before.

> **If you learn how to let go of what's in your hands, God will let go of what is in His hands.**

I have a friend from Johannesburg, South Africa. He was sharing his childhood story with me on how bad the monkeys were coming into their small village. The monkeys were stealing and destroying the crops in their fields. So, he and his friends came up with an idea on how to catch the monkeys without using a cage.

For some reason, the monkeys were too smart to get caught in a cage. So, Albu and his village friends drilled a hole within all the tree stumps and placed a banana inside of each one of them. The monkeys came out to investigate the free food. They squeezed their little hands inside the small hole to steal the banana and try to quickly run back into the jungle. The monkey resolved his food problem but developed a new problem. He needed to know how to not get caught with the banana.

I did not quite understand how they were able to catch the monkeys. My friend, Albu, explained to me how the monkeys were smart enough to steal the banana but not smart enough to become free from the tree stump. The monkeys' greed had overpowered his way of thinking. When the monkey placed his hand inside the hole of the tree stump, he made his hand small enough to where he could barely squeeze it inside the hole of the stump. However, when he gripped the banana, his hand became a fist, making it impossible to become free with the banana in hand.

The monkey needed to make a life decision. It could either let the banana go and become free or keep holding on to something that would cost him his freedom. I thought that this was a very interesting story to share with you on learning how to let go of something with no value. When you let go of those things, you become free, and God will let go of what's in his hand so that you can live in the freedom of the purpose He has carefully made for you.

Chapter 11

Seven Facts About Your Harvest That were Birthed from The Power of Your Thoughts

Often in church, I hear the people at the altar crying out before the Lord in prayer. "Oh Lord, please order my steps." Sometimes your harvest can come undisguised, and you will not recognize it when you see it. If you can't identify your first harvest, you may miss your first step.

Your life has been a parade of harvests. You must learn to recognize your harvest.

1. Your harvest could be any person or thing that could be a blessing or a benefit to you. There is a certain person in your life that you have not yet met who can contribute to something you need - information, an amazing idea, a particular favor, strength by encouragement, or financial support.

2. Your harvest was planted in your life by purpose, and every day you keep walking *around* your harvest and not recognizing it. On that special day when your eyes open and you recognize Jesus, it is the same way your eyes need to be opened to recognize your harvests.

3. Finding someone who believes in your thoughts and dreams is a harvest.

4. If you have someone who keeps recommending other people to come to you, that's a harvest. When you get a flow of favor from the people who begin to accept you, that is also considered a harvest.

5. Jesus is the Harvest of this world, and the world missed Him and received Him not. **John 1:10-11** "He was in the world, and the world was made by him, and the world knew Him not. He came unto His own, and His own receive him not." Wow! The power of pride is tragically dangerous to your soul. Religious leaders (Pharisees) and the politicians in government failed to recognize the harvest in Jesus Christ.

6. Everything that you have in your life, including your thoughts, comes from God.

7. King David said, "If I had 10,000 tongues, I would thank you with each and every last one of them." Every day, you must

take the time to celebrate God's goodness and harvest that is around you even while you sleep. Something is always working in your favor. Every day, you are continuously moving toward the harvest that is designed just for you. Pray and ask God to open up your eyes and teach you how to discern and recognize your gifts, purpose, and your harvest. If you don't plant, you will not grow, and if you don't grow, you will never receive your harvest.

Chapter 12

The Power of Agreement/ Connections

When two or three touch and agree on a thought or vision, God will order the next steps of your business plans. We need each other; don't think you can become successful on your own. God intentionally created us to have a relationship with one another. As a matter of fact, it is a command that we have a relationship with one another in business. The Bible says it is not good for man (Adam) to be alone, so he introduced partner, Eve. The void of loneliness and emptiness inside of Adam's mind and his heart became filled on that day as he would have someone bone of his bones and flesh of his flesh. It must have felt so good to Adam just to have a partner that could feel, smell, and touch the way that he did.

There are some things in the secular world you could really learn on how to build an empire. Here's a good example.

The Crips and the Bloods gangs understand the effectiveness, order, and the power of relationship. It becomes the golden link to building an empire with rules of standards.

If the gang member understands how to build effective relationships, then how much greater are you to build something from the righteousness of God?

Remember, two is always better than one because the fruit of your labor brings a greater harvest. If a partner failed in their assignment to get something accomplished, the other partners will come and lift them up.

> **Ecclesiastes 4:9-12** - *"Woe unto any man that is alone when he failed; and he does not have another brother to help him up. Again, if two lie together, and have heat: but how can one be warm alone? And if one prevails against him, two shall withstand him; and a threefold cord is not quickly broken."*

The law of assignment and connection is so powerful, and it requires two or more people to come together to be effective as partners. Nothing is more effective on Earth against the evil that keeps coming after your assignment.

> **Matthew 18:19,20.** - *"For where two or three are gathered together in* my *name, there am I in the midst of them. Amen."*

Amen.

Chapter 13

Recognition of a Golden Partnership

God can sow an idea into one man, and that same man can stand before hundreds of men and share his vision. Earlier in this book, I briefly shared about Bill Gates and his encounter in that IBM boardroom. Here are more details so that you understand the power of a Golden Partnership. Bill Gates had an idea that was rejected by a large computer company that he was working for at the time called IBM, the largest and most powerful computer corporation in communications at that time. Mr. Gates' presentation was not received by the Board of Directors, and he walked away from that prestigious group of men who had no interest in his vision. The director said to Mr. Gates, "That's impossible, and your Microsoft idea will not work in the coming future."

Three days went by, and Bill was still reeling from that meeting until he was contacted by three men from the board who actually believed in his vision. They became his key visionary **Golden Partners** that helped him and supported him in changing the world today.

I believe God will always set you up with the right people who will become your **Golden Key Partners** to help you enhance the vision He's shown you. Sometimes God will not move until you get the right partners in place. The Bible talks about the story of Simon Peter's miracle fishing experience with Jesus on the Lake of Gennesaret. Simon

Peter and his partners had been fishing all night and had not caught one fish. Jesus asked Simon Peter to cast out his net on the right side of the boat, which Peter did. The Bible said a great multitude of fish swam inside of that net, causing it to break. At the shocking surprise of the increase of more than enough, Peter's **Golden Key Partners,** James and John, the sons of Zebedee, saw that business was booming and cast their nets into the water to keep as much fish as they could.

This biblical story shows the importance of having the right partners in place so that when God increases your business or ministry, you are ready with the right partners around you. At any given time, someone may need your service in large quantities, so you must have the right partners in place to assist you in meeting the needs of others. I would encourage you to read the entire story in your leisure time. It can be found in Luke 5:1-10.

Final Thoughts Before You Take Action

The secret of the power of thought comes from the power of faith. If you don't experience trouble, you will never be introduced to faith - the faith of God. The Bible tells us that in the time of trouble is when He shows up. So, if we don't have any trouble, we will never have an encounter with God coming to our rescue. That builds up my thoughts because faith has always been the secret to the enhancement of my thoughts. So, stop getting weary and troubled when things don't go your way, or you are being spiritually attacked. Sit back in your spiritual recliner and ask God to give you the solution to what is going on with your friends and family so you can help solve it. You have not because you ask not. God will give you the power over your thoughts. If you can't control your thoughts, you will never have power. Control your thoughts! If you can't control your thoughts, you can't control your vision. Overcome the dumbness!

I want to leave you with three things to consider as I close out this book, and then it will be time for you to take action.

Number 1: Do you have control of your thoughts? The Word says an unstable man is wavering in all of his thoughts. His thoughts are like the wind. Wherever the wind goes, that's where his thoughts go. **James 1:8.**

Number 2: Identify your gift. Look behind your purpose. If you don't look behind your purpose, you won't find your gift. What do you keep doing that everyone keeps coming to you asking if you can do that for them?

Number 3: Are you leading with your gift and purpose? If you let someone else dictate what you should do and which way you should go, then you are not leading, you are simply following, and leaders have power over their own thoughts.

It's time for you to take action: Choose one nugget of wisdom that I shared in each chapter. Focus on that nugget and outline how you will reclaim the power of your own thoughts in that particular area.

If you take the time and study the steps that I've placed in this book for you, you can overcome anything in your life through

Christ Jesus. May God bless you and know that our success is through Christ.

CPSIA information can be obtained
at www.ICGtesting.com
Printed in the USA
JSHW050155220920
7807JS00019B/47